Step-by-Step
Creative Lettering

Judy Balchin

Search Press

First published in Great Britain 2001

Search Press Limited
Wellwood, North Farm Road,
Tunbridge Wells, Kent TN2 3DR

Reprinted 2002, 2004, 2005

Text copyright © Judy Balchin 2001

Photographs by Search Press Studios
Photographs and design copyright © Search Press Ltd.
2001

ISBN 0 85532 907 6

Suppliers
If you have difficulty in obtaining any of the materials and
equipment mentioned in this book, then please visit the
Search Press website for details of suppliers:
www.searchpress.com

Alternatively, you can write to the Publishers at the
address above, for a current list of stockists, which
includes firms who operate a mail-order service.

Acknowledgements
The Publishers would like to thank the Bridgeman Art
Library for permission to reproduce the photograph on
page 5.

Colour separation by Graphics '91 Pte Ltd., Singapore
Printed in China by WKT Company Ltd

To Uncle Bill

*Special thanks to Mr Kaoru Osaki of
Kuretake UK Ltd, 6 Colemeadow Road,
North Moons Moat, Redditch, Worcestershire
B98 6PB, for supplying the ZIG pens used in
this book. Many thanks are also due to all at
Search Press. Their professional yet friendly
team made writing this book a pleasure. In
particular, thanks to Editorial Director Roz
Dace, for her guidance; Editor Chantal Roser
for her vision; Designer Tamsin Hayes for
her creative design skills and photographer
Lotti de la Bédoyère for her patience and
attention to detail.*

*The Publishers would like to say a huge
thank you to Charlotte Palmer-Joy,
Abu Subhan, Chris Fields, Emily Malins and
Rupert Malins.*

*Special thanks are also due to Southborough
Primary School, Tunbridge Wells.*

When this sign is used in the
book, it means that adult
supervision is needed.

REMEMBER!
Ask an adult to help you when
you see this sign.

Contents

Introduction

Imagine a world with no letters – no books, signs or labels, no way to leave a message for your parents or to write to friends. Well, that is how it was a long time ago. There were no letters; they actually had to be invented.

Many years ago the American Indians used pictures called pictograms as a memory guide to remind them of events and songs when telling stories. As time went on and more complicated information needed to be exchanged or remembered, symbols were created to represent ideas or things. We can still see this today in the Chinese alphabet. Every idea or thing has its own symbol and believe it or not, a Chinese scholar must know over fifteen thousand symbols to write his books. The ancient Egyptians used another complicated system called hieroglyphics. We all know our ABC, but did you know that the letter A was once a hieroglyphic symbol of an eagle and B was a crane?

Over time, alphabets had to change and become simpler. The first simple alphabet was invented in Assyria in the fourteenth century BC. It was called cuneiform and was made up of lines and wedge shapes. It had thirty letters and was used by merchants to record their business dealings. The twenty-six letters we use today are derived from the Greek alphabet. In fact the word 'alphabet' is made from the first two letters of the Greek alphabet, alpha and beta.

We are surrounded by letters. Advertisers are extremely competitive and creative with their lettering styles as they entice you to buy their product. Perhaps you could try having a 'letter awareness' day. Get up in the morning, brush your teeth and look at the lettering on your toothpaste tube. Read the cereal packet over breakfast and see what letters are used. Look at book covers at school and while you eat your lunch, study the food wrappers. Television too offers us a variety of letter styles. It is amazing just how creative you can be with letters.

Now that you know the wonderful history of the alphabet and just how important lettering is to our everyday lives, we can have some fun. By the time you have worked your way through this book you will be able to tell the difference between 'serif' and 'sans serif' letters. You will notice 'drop shadows' on letters and begin to understand how important colour is. With a few pens and some paper you will be able to create your own letters and make cards, invitations, writing paper, bookmarks, posters and much more. I hope that this book inspires you to continue with this fascinating hobby.

__Opposite__ This colourful page from a Book of Hours was written and illustrated in Italy in about 1500 AD. The large letter D has been decorated with leaves and a picture of King David at prayer. Books of Hours contained pictures and short prayers – each suitable for a particular hour of the day. They became so popular that artists had to employ many assistants to help them produce enough books.

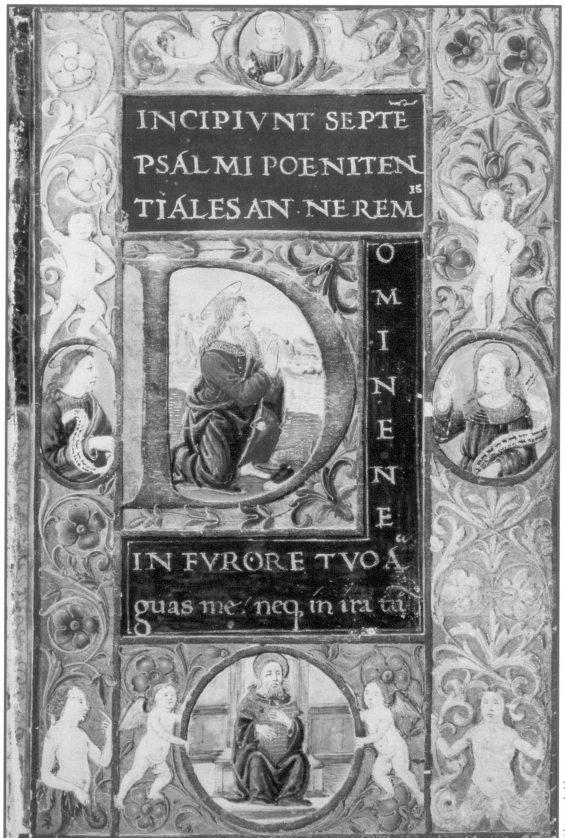

INCIPIVNT SEPTE
PSALMI POENITEN
TIALES AN·NE REM
DOMINE·N·E
IN FVRORE TVO A
guas me: neq, in ira tu

5

Materials

The items pictured on these pages are the basic equipment you might need for creative lettering. You may already have some of them at home, but other items are easy to buy from local art shops. In addition, there are some specific items needed for certain projects, such as ribbons, a hole punch, a round cardboard box and a coloured folder.

Note Whenever you use paints or pens, you should cover your working area with newspaper. Wear old clothes and work on a tidy, flat surface. Have a damp cloth at the ready in case of spills.

All sorts of **card** and **paper** can be used for creative lettering – from white and coloured paper to metallic, sparkly and coloured card.

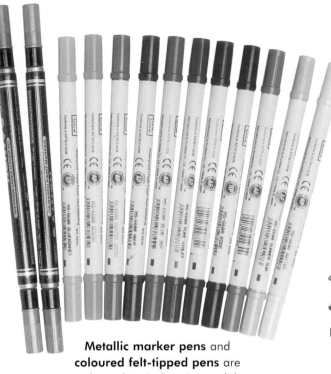

Metallic marker pens and **coloured felt-tipped pens** are used to colour in lettering and the edges of boxes.

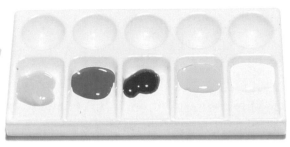

The paint used in this book is **water-based** and **acrylic**. It is best to use paint from a **palette** rather than straight from the pot.

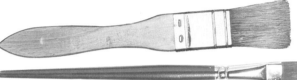

Paint is applied with **paintbrushes**.

Pencil lines are rubbed out with an **eraser**.

Scissors are used to cut paper, card and ribbon.

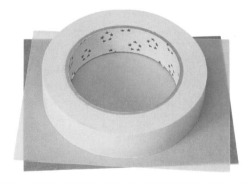

Transfer paper, **tracing paper** and a **pencil** are used when transferring or tracing designs. **Masking tape** is used to hold the designs in place.

PVA glue is used to stick surfaces together.

Neat round holes are made with a **hole punch**.

A **ruler** is used for drawing straight lines.

Techniques

Take time to read through this techniques section before you start the projects. The alphabets and patterns that you will need are on pages 26–31. You can transfer them on to your paper with transfer paper.

Ask an adult to help you enlarge the letters and patterns on a photocopier.

Transferring letters and patterns

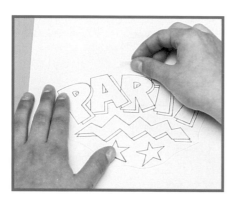

 Enlarge the pattern on a photocopier and cut it out. Lay it on a sheet of paper and tape the top with a piece of masking tape.

 Slip the transfer paper face-down under the pattern and tape it at the bottom to keep it in place.

 Trace around the outline of the pattern with a pencil to transfer the design on to the paper.

 Remove the transfer paper, then go over the outline with a black pen. Leave to dry for five minutes.

 Rub out any lines or smudges with an eraser and fill in the design with coloured pens.

Note Remember to put the tops back on your pens.

Copying letters

You will be asked to copy letters from the alphabets at the back of the book. Planning your lettering is important. Always work in pencil before going over the letters with a pen.

 Lightly draw in the guidelines for the lettering. A guideline is the line on which your letters sit. It may be straight, curved or wavy.

Note Cut a star shape around the design, or choose your own shape.

2 Pencil in the letters using the alphabet as a guide (see page 26). This dot serif alphabet is the easiest one to start with as it is based on neat writing.

3 Go over the pencilled letters with a coloured pen, adding dots to the ends and joints of the letters. When the pen has dried, remove any visible pencil lines with an eraser.

Rocket Birthday Card

Make your own dazzling range of cards using coloured pens and paper. The 'dot serif' alphabet used here is the easiest alphabet to create. All you have to do is print your message clearly, then add dots to the ends and joints of the letters. You can bring a sense of movement into the words by slanting the letters in different ways. A pattern has been provided (see page 31), but you might like to try this project without using the pattern. Practise on scrap paper first.

YOU WILL NEED

White paper
Coloured felt-tipped pens
Metallic card • Black felt-tipped pen
Metallic marker pen
Transfer paper • Masking tape
Pencil • Eraser • Scissors
PVA glue

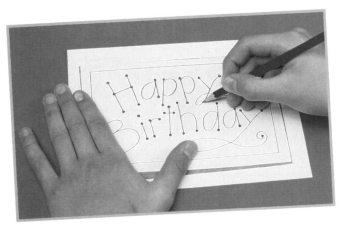

1 Transfer the pattern from page 31 on to white paper (see page 8).

2 Go over the outlines with a black felt-tipped pen. Leave to dry then rub out all the pencil lines.

3 Run a coloured line around the black lettering.

4 Colour in the rocket, then use a metallic pen to decorate it with two rows of dots. Draw stars between the letters to fill in any spaces.

5 Cut out the design.

6 Fold a sheet of metallic card in half and glue your design in place.

FURTHER IDEAS
You can create lots of cards for other occasions. Decorate them with colourful shapes and images.

Balloon Party Invitation

Send a special party invitation to your friends. A 'sans serif' alphabet with a 'drop shadow' is used for the lettering. Serifs are the lines that extend across the ends of the letters and 'Sans serif' means without serifs. Compare the alphabets on pages 28 and 29 to see the difference between 'serif' and 'sans serif' letters. A 'drop shadow' is a thick line which is usually drawn down one side and along the bottom of a letter, which makes it really stand out. This type of lettering is often used on food and sweet wrappers as it is bold and eye-catching.

YOU WILL NEED

Coloured card
Coloured felt-tipped pens
Black felt-tipped pen
Curling ribbon • Transfer paper
Masking tape • Pencil
Scissors • Eraser

1 Transfer the basic pattern from page 31 on to coloured card (see page 8). Go over the outline of the letters and designs with a black felt-tipped pen. Fill in the drop shadow.

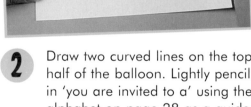

2 Draw two curved lines on the top half of the balloon. Lightly pencil in 'you are invited to a' using the alphabet on page 28 as a guide.

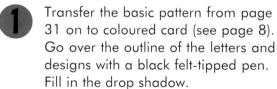

3 Outline the lettering with a brightly coloured pen. Leave to dry for a few minutes, then rub out any visible pencil lines.

Fill in the word 'party' and the zig-zag shape underneath with the same colour. Fill in the stars using a different colour, then add some curly lines.

5 Cut out the invitation. Tie a piece of paper ribbon around the knot of the balloon.

6 Lightly pencil in some guidelines on the back of the invitation, then write down your message.

FURTHER IDEAS
Write your name in the balloon and fill in the letters with lots of different colours.

Alien Door Plaque

A design can look fun if you combine an illustration with the lettering and then decorate each letter with different colours and patterns. The door plaque uses the 'line serif' alphabet on page 29, where lines are drawn across the ends of the letters, so that they extend slightly beyond the letter. Can you spot 'serif' letters in your books?

YOU WILL NEED
White card
Black felt-tipped pen
Coloured felt-tipped pens
Transfer paper • Masking tape
Pencil • Eraser
Scissors

 Transfer the pattern shown on page 31 on to white card (see page 8), then go over the outline with a black felt-tipped pen. Leave to dry.

 Fill in each of the letters with a different design. Use lots of colours.

 Use the dot serif alphabet on page 26 to pencil in 'my room' underneath and then outline with a coloured pen. Leave to dry and rub out all the pencil lines.

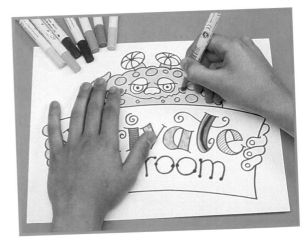

 Colour in the alien.

5 Draw a coloured border around the panel.

6 Cut out the plaque, leaving a small border around the edge.

FURTHER IDEAS

Use another alphabet and different colours to personalise a journal, school book or notebook.

Ask an adult to help you attach the plaque to your door. You can use low-tack masking tape or removable adhesive.

Illuminated Bookmark

The inspiration for this project is taken from beautifully illuminated old manuscripts. These were created by monks using quill pens and paints, and the first capital letter on a page was always decorated with gold leaf and bright colours. Water-based paint and a metallic marker pen are used to create an illuminated bookmark. Use a dark colour for your own initial so that the metallic pen work really stands out.

YOU WILL NEED

Dark coloured card
Light coloured paper
Metallic marker pen
Water-based paint • Small paintbrush
Transfer paper • Masking Tape
Pencil • Eraser • Ruler
Scissors • PVA glue
Hole punch • Ribbon

1 Transfer a letter from the alphabet on page 27 on to light coloured paper (see page 8). Paint it using a dark colour. Leave to dry.

2 Use the alphabet pattern as a guide. Outline the letter and swirls with a metallic marker pen. Draw the inner lines. Leave to dry.

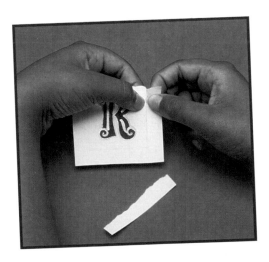

3 With a ruler and pencil, draw a square around the letter. Cut around the square leaving a small border, then tear the edges following the lines.

Draw a rectangle on dark card and tear the edges. Colour the edges of the square and the rectangle with a metallic marker pen.

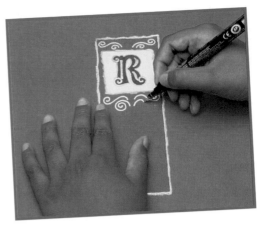

Thread the bookmark with matching ribbon. Fold the ribbon in half, push the loop through the hole and pull the ends through the loop.

5 Punch a hole at the top of the rectangle with a hole punch and glue the letter below it. Add swirls around the square with the metallic pen, then transfer the pattern shown on page 31 on to the area below the letter (see page 8).

FURTHER IDEAS

By changing the initial and the colours you can make bookmarks for all your friends.

Personalised Paper

Creating your own personalised writing paper will give your letters a distinctive look. The letters are drawn in boxes which are cut out, arranged on a sheet of paper, then glued into place. The design can be photocopied many times and each copy can then be decorated with colours and motifs of your choice.

YOU WILL NEED

White paper
Black felt-tipped pen
Coloured felt-tipped pens
Ruler • Pencil
Scissors • PVA glue

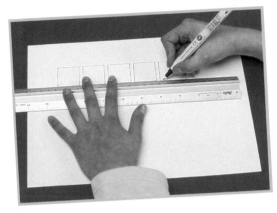

1 Count the letters in your first name. Draw the same number of 3cm (1¼in) squares on a piece of paper and outline them with a black felt-tipped pen.

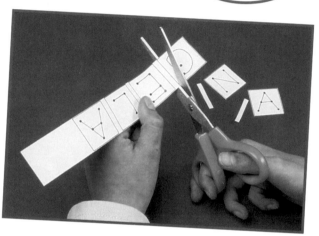

2 Choose an alphabet from the back of the book (see pages 26-30). Use a pencil to copy each letter of your name on to a square. Go over the outline of the letters with a black felt-tipped pen. Leave to dry, rub out any visible pencil lines, then cut out the squares.

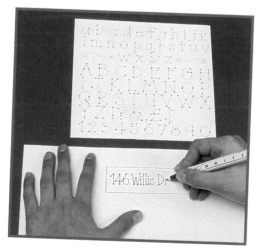

3 Draw a rectangle 3cm x 9cm (1¼in x 3¾in) and outline it in black. Write your address within it and then cut out the rectangle.

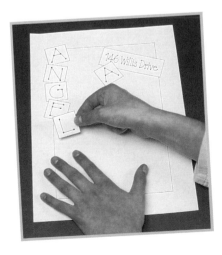

4 Use a ruler to draw a border line 3 cm (1¼in) from the edges of a sheet of white paper. Glue the squares down the left-hand edge of the border, then glue the rectangle in the bottom right-hand corner.

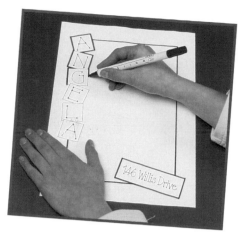

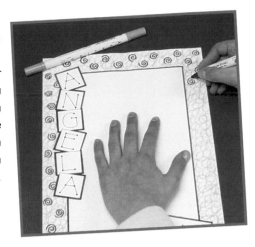

6

Cover the outer border with a swirling pattern using a pale colour, then decorate it with darker spirals.

5

Photocopy your letterhead as many times as you wish. Edge the border, the address panel and each square with a coloured pen.

(!)

Ask an adult to help you photocopy the letterhead.

FURTHER IDEAS

Choose a different alphabet and photocopy your design on to coloured paper. Decorate the border with squares, triangles or circles.

Snow White Poster

Large letters and bright colours are needed for a title when you are making a poster. This makes it more eye-catching. It is easier to cut the letters out of paper and to arrange them on a card base along with an information panel. When you are satisfied with the design, glue all the letters down.

YOU WILL NEED

Coloured and white paper
Sparkly card
Coloured card
Tracing paper • Pencil
Coloured felt-tipped pens
Scissors • PVA glue

(!)

Ask an adult to help you enlarge the letters on a photocopier.

 Trace the letters for the title using the alphabet on page 30. Enlarge the letters on a photocopier so that the longest word fits comfortably across a sheet of paper. Cut the letters out.

2 Lay the letters on the sparkly card and draw around them.

3

Cut the letters out and arrange them across the top of the coloured card. Glue them in position. Cut and glue a rectangle of sparkly card to fit within the bottom half of the card.

 4

Cut out a piece of white paper slightly smaller than the rectangle of sparkly card. Using the letters on page 26 as a guide, pencil your message on to the white rectangle. Go over the words with coloured pens.

 5

Glue the panel on to the sparkly card.

 6

Cut out stars from coloured paper and glue them around the edge of your poster.

FURTHER IDEAS

Make more posters to broadcast special messages or school news. Illustrate them with different shapes and patterns.

Hobby Box

The style and decoration of lettering tells us quite a lot. This container needs a bold, brightly coloured label which shouts 'paints'. The letters have a drop shadow and are overlapped slightly to give them a three dimensional look. The colours of the box and label complement each other, which creates a bright, stylish look.

YOU WILL NEED

Round cardboard box 16cm diameter x 10cm high (6¼in x 4in)
White paper • Pencil
Black felt-tipped pen
Coloured felt-tipped pens • Scissors
Acrylic paints
Small and large paintbrushes
PVA glue

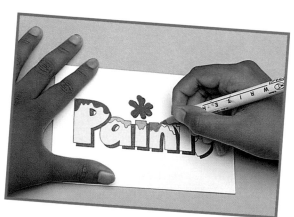

1 Draw the guidelines on white paper with a pencil. Copy the word 'Paints' using the alphabet on page 28 as a guide. Replace the dot over the 'i' with a splash shape, then add a drop shadow to the splash.

2 Use a black felt-tipped pen to go over the outlines of the letters, then fill in the drop shadow. Run wavy lines along the top of the letters to look like dripping paint.

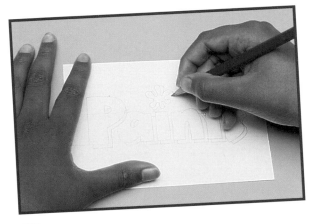

3 Fill in the letters with a bright colour, then fill in the splash and drips with different colours.

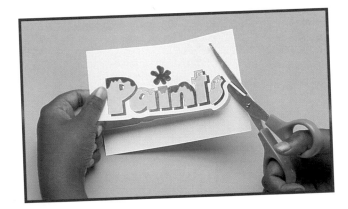

4 Cut around the letters, leaving a 0.5cm (¼in) border of white paper.

5 Use acrylic paints and a large paintbrush to paint the box and lid with bright colours. Draw splash shapes over the lid with a black felt-tipped pen. Leave to dry, then paint them in with bright colours using a small paintbrush.

6 Glue the finished label to the front of the box.

FURTHER IDEAS
Make a jewellery box using pastel colours and sparkly letters, or a treasure box using metallic colours.

School Project Folder

By now you will be getting more confident with your lettering. This project is great fun and you can really be creative! Each letter is transformed into an illustration. The first letter is 'P' – and P is for pencil, so you could draw a pencil in the shape of the letter P. The next letter is 'R' and R is for ribbon. Try to think of different things for each letter in the word 'Project'.

YOU WILL NEED

Coloured folder
Pencil • Ruler
White paper
Black felt-tipped pen
Coloured felt-tipped pens
PVA glue

1

Spend a little time planning what you want the letters to be. Write them down on a piece of paper and alongside each one make a list of things beginning with that letter. Try drawing a few of them to see how they will look.

2 Use a pencil and ruler to draw seven 6cm (2¼in) squares on a piece of white paper. Leave a gap of about 3cm (1¼in) between the squares.

3 Use a pencil and draw one illustrated letter on each square.

4 Go over the outlines of each letter with a black felt-tipped pen, then fill them in with different colours.

 5

Cut around each box, leaving a small border. Now tear the edges of the squares following the lines.

 6 Place the torn squares on a scrap piece of paper. Add a coloured border around the edges of each square.

7

Arrange the squares on your folder, then glue them into place.

FURTHER IDEAS

Create an alphabet using a different animal for each letter, or decorate your folder with fantasy figures.

Alphabets

These alphabets can be copied or traced on to tracing paper, then transferred on to your writing surface with transfer paper. They can also be enlarged on a photocopier if you are making a poster.

If you want to photocopy these letters, ask an adult to help you.

Dot serif

Readers are allowed to photocopy the patterns in this book for their personal use free of charge and without prior permission of the publishers.

Illuminated

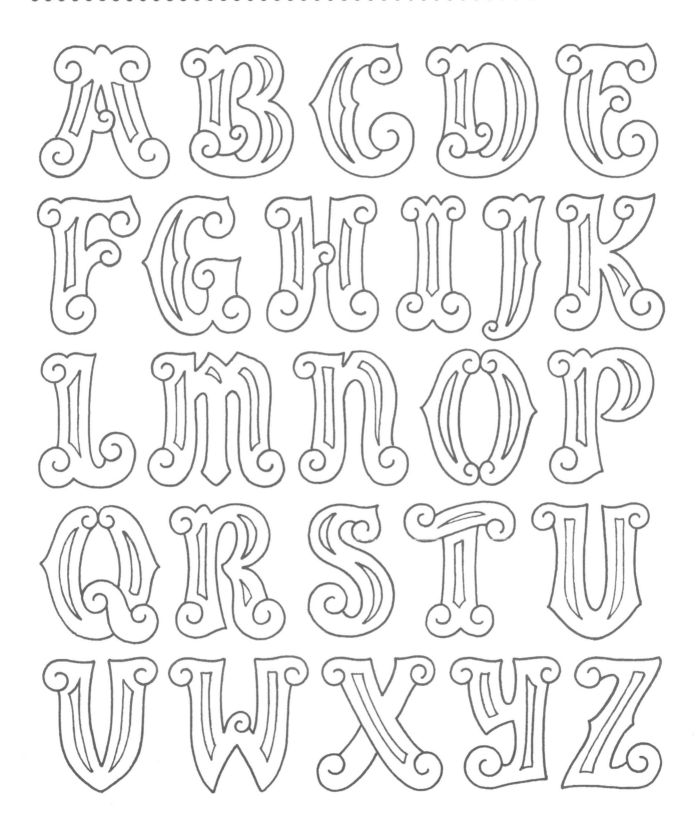

Block sans serif with drop shadow

abcdefghij
klmnopqrs
tuvwxyz

ABCDEFG
HIJKLMN
OPQRSTU
VWXYZ!?&,£$

1234567890

Line serif

abcdefghij
klmnopqrs
tuvwxyz
ABCDEFG
HIJKLMN
OPQRSTUV
WXYZ!?&£$
1234567890

Rounded sans serif

a b c d e f g h i
j k l m n o p q r
s t u v w x y z

A B C D E F G H
I J K L M N O P
Q R S T U V W
X Y Z ! ? & , £ $
1 2 3 4 5 6 7 8 9 0

Patterns

Ask an adult to help you enlarge the patterns on a photocopier.

Pattern for the Alien Door Plaque featured on pages 14–15.

Pattern for the Illuminated Bookmark featured on pages 16–17.

Pattern for the Balloon Party Invitation featured on pages 12–13.

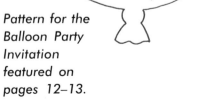

Pattern for the Rocket Birthday Card featured on pages 10–11.

Index